I0698572

Title: "Coding the Cosmos:A Journey

Through Time, Quantum, and Beyond"

Table

of

contents:

Chapter 1: "The Genesis Code" In this chapter, we explore the idea of a new year resolution in the context of coding the future. Introduce the concept of a unique coding language, "ChronoScript," that concatenates the past and present worlds, weaving a narrative through time. Discuss the significance of setting ambitious goals for the future and how ChronoScript can be a tool for transformation.

Chapter 2: "Unraveling the Quantum Code" Delve into the potential of quantum machine learning as the next technological revolution. Explain the basic principles of quantum computing and its applications in coding and solving complex problems. Explore the possibilities of a new quantum coding language, "QuantumScript," and how it might reshape the landscape of programming.

Chapter 3: "Deciphering the Unknown" Introduce the notion of undiscovered coding languages, languages that are yet to be deciphered by the coding community. Discuss the excitement of exploring the unknown and the potential breakthroughs that could emerge from decoding these mysterious languages. Highlight the importance of curiosity and innovation in the world of coding.

Chapter 4: "Brightening the Present" Shift the focus to the present world and how coding can contribute to making a positive impact. Explore real-world examples of how technology and coding have been used to address current challenges, from environmental issues to social justice. Discuss how the skills acquired through learning future coding languages can be applied to create a brighter and more sustainable present.

Chapter 5: "The Theory of Universe in Code" Wrap up the book by connecting coding with the grand theory of the universe. Discuss the parallels between the structure of the cosmos and the logic of coding languages. Explore the idea that the universe itself may be a vast, intricate code waiting to be deciphered. Conclude with a call to action for readers to continue exploring the limitless possibilities of coding and understanding the universe through the lens of ChronoScript, QuantumScript, and the languages yet to be discovered.

Through this book, readers will embark on a thought-provoking journey that connects the past, present, and future of coding, while also exploring the mysteries of the universe in a code-driven narrative.

Chapter 1:
"The

Genesis Code"

As the clock strikes midnight, marking the beginning of a new year, the air is filled with a sense of anticipation and the promise of new beginnings. Many of us embark on this journey armed with resolutions, a commitment to change, grow, and shape our future. In the world of coding, a parallel journey unfolds—one that seeks to not only set resolutions but to code the very fabric of the future itself.

The Call of Resolution

In the opening pages of this chapter, we delve into the timeless tradition of making New Year resolutions. We explore the psychology behind setting goals, the motivation that fuels them, and the significance of this annual ritual in shaping individual destinies. It's a moment when individuals pause to reflect on the past, acknowledge the present, and cast their aspirations into the future.

The Birth of ChronoScript

Amidst the backdrop of this age-old tradition, a new concept emerges—the genesis of a unique coding language known as "ChronoScript." This language transcends the boundaries of traditional programming by weaving a narrative that concatenates the past and the present. The reader is introduced to the core principles of ChronoScript and how it functions as a temporal bridge, allowing coders to navigate through different eras in the code.

Coding Through Time

ChronoScript enables programmers to tap into the wisdom of the past while leveraging the innovations of the present. We explore how this fusion of historical knowledge and contemporary technology empowers coders to *create solutions that stand the test of time. Through illustrative examples, we showcase how ChronoScript can be a transformative tool, not just for coding, but for shaping one's life and the world around us.*

Ambitious Goals in Code

The narrative then shifts to the power of ambition and the significance of setting audacious goals for the future. We discuss how coding, infused with the spirit of resolution, can transcend the ordinary and reach new heights. The language of ChronoScript becomes a vessel for these ambitions, providing a medium to articulate and manifest the dreams that define the future.

Transformation Through ChronoScript

The final section of the chapter explores how ChronoScript can be a catalyst for personal and collective transformation. We delve into real-world examples of individuals and organizations that have embraced this coding language to reimagine their future. From reinvigorating outdated systems to launching groundbreaking projects, ChronoScript becomes a tool for not just coding but for sculpting a future that aligns with one's deepest aspirations.

Conclusion: Beyond the Threshold of Time

As the first chapter concludes, readers are left at the threshold of time, contemplating the possibilities embedded in the Genesis Code. The journey has just begun, and the pages of the book turn with the promise of unveiling more about ChronoScript, ambitious coding goals, and the transformative power of coding the future. The reader is invited to venture further into this exploration, armed with the understanding that the language of coding is not merely a set of instructions but a dynamic force that can shape the very fabric of our existence.

Chapter 2: "Unraveling the

Quantum Code"

Introduction:

Quantum Dawn

In the realm of coding, a new dawn is breaking—a quantum dawn. As we venture deeper into the second chapter, we transition from the temporal tapestry of ChronoScript to the cutting-edge world of quantum computing. The quest for innovation and the thirst for knowledge lead us to the forefront of technological revolution—the quantum code.

The Quantum Leap

The journey commences with an exploration of the fundamental principles of quantum computing. We unravel the mysteries of qubits, quantum entanglement, and superposition, laying the groundwork for understanding how *these quantum phenomena diverge from classical computing. Through vivid explanations and analogies, the chapter seeks to demystify the complex nature of quantum mechanics for both seasoned coders and those new to the quantum realm.*

Quantum Machine Learning: A Symbiotic Alliance

The narrative then seamlessly shifts to the convergence of quantum computing and machine learning. We delve into the symbiotic relationship between these two transformative fields, exploring how the inherent parallelism and computational power of quantum systems can revolutionize the way we approach complex problem-solving in machine learning. Real-world examples illustrate how quantum machine learning algorithms can outpace classical counterparts, unlocking unprecedented possibilities.

QuantumScript: Coding in a Parallel Universe

As the chapter unfolds, a new language emerges—QuantumScript. We embark on an exploration of the syntax, structure, and unique features that define this quantum coding language. Through code snippets and examples, readers gain insights into how QuantumScript harnesses the power of quantum computing, offering a glimpse into a programming paradigm that transcends the limitations of classical binary code.

Reshaping the Landscape of Programming

The spotlight then turns to the broader implications of QuantumScript on the programming landscape. We examine how quantum computing can disrupt traditional approaches to problem-solving, cryptography, and optimization. The chapter explores the potential impact on industries ranging from finance to healthcare, underscoring the transformative nature of quantum code in shaping the future of technology.

Challenges and Ethical Considerations

No exploration of revolutionary technologies is complete without acknowledging the challenges and ethical considerations they pose. In this section, we confront the limitations and uncertainties surrounding quantum computing, addressing issues such as error correction, scalability, and the societal impact of quantum advancements. The reader is encouraged to contemplate the ethical dimensions of wielding such powerful tools in the coding universe.

Conclusion: Quantum Horizons

As the Quantum Code chapter draws to a close, readers find themselves standing at the precipice of quantum horizons. The potential of QuantumScript and quantum computing looms large, offering a glimpse into a future where the boundaries of classical computation are surpassed. The chapter serves as an invitation for coders to venture further into the quantum realm, where the code takes on a dimension beyond the binary, and the promise of transformative possibilities awaits those willing to unravel the quantum code.

Chapter 3: "Decipheri

ng the
Unknown"

**Introducti
on: The
Enigma**

# of Uncharted Code

In the vast landscape of coding, where languages have flourished and evolved, a new frontier awaits—uncharted territories filled with the promise of undiscovered coding languages. As we embark on the third chapter, the air is charged with excitement, curiosity, and the anticipation of breakthroughs yet to come.

The Unknown Tongues of Code

The chapter begins by laying the groundwork for the concept of undiscovered coding languages. We delve into the rich history of programming languages, acknowledging the pioneers who laid the foundations and the multitude of languages that have shaped the coding landscape. Against this backdrop, the notion of undiscovered languages emerges, hinting at a treasure trove of knowledge waiting to be unearthed.

The Allure of Mystery

The narrative then explores the allure of the unknown in the world of coding. We discuss the innate human fascination with mysteries and how it drives innovation. Through anecdotes and historical examples, readers are immersed in the thrill of discovery and the joy of unraveling the enigmatic threads of previously unknown coding languages.

Unveiling the Potential Breakthroughs

The heart of the chapter lies in the exploration of potential breakthroughs that could emerge from deciphering these mysterious languages. We examine the theoretical foundations, computational challenges, and real-world applications that might be unlocked through the understanding of languages previously hidden from the coding community. Interviews with leading researchers and thinkers provide insights into the transformative possibilities that await those who dare to decipher the unknown.

The Dance of Curiosity and Innovation

A spotlight is then cast on the symbiotic relationship between curiosity and innovation in the coding world. We explore how the insatiable curiosity of coders propels them to venture into the unknown, seeking to unravel the mysteries of these undiscovered languages. Through case studies and success stories, we showcase how curiosity-driven exploration leads to innovative solutions and pushes the boundaries of what is deemed possible.

The Human Element in Decoding

The narrative takes a humanistic turn as we delve into the role of the coder as an explorer. The importance of intuition, creativity, and collaborative efforts in deciphering unknown languages is emphasized. We explore the interconnectedness of the coding community, where diverse perspectives and collective intelligence become powerful tools in the quest for decoding the unknown.

Conclusion: The Tapestry of Tomorrow's Code

As the chapter concludes, readers are left with a sense of awe and inspiration. The allure of undiscovered coding languages beckons, and the excitement of decoding the unknown becomes a driving force for innovation. The chapter serves as a reminder that, in the ever-evolving world of coding, the journey into uncharted territories is as essential as the knowledge we've already acquired. It is a call to embrace the mysteries, to cherish the thrill of discovery, and to recognize that the tapestry of tomorrow's code is woven with threads that are yet to be unveiled.

Chapter 4: "Brightening the Present"

Introduction: The Code of Impact

As the journey through the coding cosmos unfolds, we find ourselves in the vibrant realm of the present—where the lines of code written today have the power to shape a brighter and more sustainable world. In this chapter, we shift our focus to the transformative potential of *coding in addressing contemporary challenges and bringing positive change.*

Coding for a Cause

The chapter commences by exploring the concept of coding with a purpose. We delve into the idea that programming is not just about crafting algorithms and applications but also about using these skills to contribute meaningfully to society. Real-world examples of coding projects geared towards social impact are examined, highlighting how technology can be a force for positive change.

Environmental Stewardship through Code

The narrative then transitions to the urgent global issue of environmental sustainability. We showcase instances where coding has been employed to monitor and mitigate environmental challenges, from climate change to conservation efforts. Through case studies and interviews with environmental tech innovators, readers gain insights into the profound impact that code can have on our planet's well-being.

Coding for Social Justice

The spotlight turns to the realm of social justice, where coding emerges as a tool for equality and empowerment. The chapter explores initiatives that leverage technology to address issues such as access to education, healthcare, and social services. Through the lens of coding, readers witness how innovative solutions are being developed to bridge gaps and uplift marginalized communities.

Tech for Good: Humanitarian Coding

The narrative widens to encompass humanitarian efforts, where coding becomes a lifeline in crisis situations. We examine how technology, including advanced coding languages, plays a crucial role in disaster response, refugee support, and global health crises. The chapter emphasizes the power of coding not just as a technical skill but as a force for human resilience and compassion.

The Synergy of Future Code

Building on the foundation of current coding practices, the chapter explores how skills acquired through learning future coding languages can amplify the impact of technological interventions. We discuss the synergies between ChronoScript, QuantumScript, and other cutting-edge languages, showcasing how these tools can be harnessed to create solutions that are not only innovative but also future-proof.

Empowering Individuals Through Code

The narrative takes a personal turn as we highlight stories of individuals who, armed with coding skills, have made a positive impact on their communities. From grassroots initiatives to global movements, readers witness the transformative potential of coding in the hands of passionate individuals. The chapter encourages readers to see themselves as agents of change, equipped with the tools to contribute to a brighter present.

Conclusion: Code as a Catalyst

As the chapter draws to a close, readers are left with a profound understanding of the catalytic role that coding plays in brightening the present. The journey through real-world examples, challenges addressed, and lives impacted underscores the potential for coding to be a force for good. It is an invitation for every coder to recognize their capacity to contribute to a more sustainable and equitable world through the art and science of programming. In the coding cosmos, the present is not just a moment in time but an opportunity to make a lasting impact.

Chapter 5: "The Theory of Universe in Code"

Introduction: Code and Cosmos

As we reach the final chapter of our journey through the coding cosmos, we venture into the profound and speculative realms where code and the universe converge. The chapter seeks to weave a tapestry of connections between the intricate structures of the cosmos and the *logical frameworks of coding languages. It invites readers to ponder the tantalizing possibility that the universe itself may be a vast and complex code awaiting decipherment.*

The Elegant Code of Nature

The journey begins by exploring the elegance and order inherent in the universe. We delve into the fundamental principles that govern the cosmos, drawing parallels with the structured syntax of coding languages. The reader is introduced to the idea that the laws of physics and the mathematical equations that describe the universe can be seen as a form of cosmic code—a code that governs the behavior of matter, energy, and the very fabric of space-time.

Coding the Cosmos: A Cosmic Script

The narrative unfolds to discuss the notion that the universe might be expressing itself through a grand cosmic script. Drawing inspiration from ChronoScript and QuantumScript, the chapter postulates the existence of a cosmic language—

a script that encapsulates the entire history of the universe, from its mysterious origins to its expansive future. The reader is encouraged to imagine the cosmic narrative written in a code that transcends human understanding.

The Universe as a Computational Entity

An exploration of the universe as a computational entity ensues. The chapter delves into theoretical frameworks like digital physics, proposing that at the most fundamental level, the universe operates as a vast quantum computer. We examine the parallels between the computations carried out in coding languages and the underlying processes that drive the dynamics of the cosmos.

Deciphering the Cosmic Code

The narrative takes an adventurous turn as we entertain the idea of deciphering the cosmic code. Drawing inspiration from the curiosity-

driven exploration discussed in earlier chapters, the reader is invited to ponder whether humanity, armed with advanced coding languages, might one day unravel the mysteries of the universe. The potential implications of deciphering the cosmic code are explored, from unlocking the secrets of dark matter to understanding the very nature of reality.

A Call to Explore: Beyond the Known and Unknown

The chapter concludes with a resounding call to action for readers. As we reflect on the parallels between coding and the universe, we recognize that the journey is far from over. The call is not just to explore the known languages like ChronoScript and QuantumScript but to embrace the spirit of curiosity and innovation in the face of the unknown. The reader is encouraged to continue the exploration of coding languages, both established and undiscovered, as a means to deepen our understanding of the universe and our place within it.

Epilogue: Beyond the Coding Cosmos

The final pages of the chapter serve as an epilogue to the entire book. The reader is left with a sense of awe and wonder, contemplating the interconnectedness of code and the cosmos. It is a reminder that the coding cosmos is an ever-expanding frontier, full of mysteries waiting to be unraveled. As the book concludes, the reader is invited to carry the spirit of exploration and the understanding gained into their own coding endeavors, inspiring them to be pioneers in the uncharted territories of both code and the universe. The journey continues, and the possibilities are limitless.

Let's dive into

coding part:

Chapter 1: "The

Genesis Code"

Introducti on: Coding

Resolutions for a New Epoch

As the calendar turns its page to a new year, the air is thick with the promise of fresh starts and ambitious resolutions. In the world of coding, this chapter invites readers to transcend the ordinary and envision a future shaped by the unique coding language, "ChronoScript." Here, we explore the profound intersection of time, ambition, and transformation within the realm of coding.

Setting the Stage for Ambition

The opening pages delve into the psychology of setting resolutions, emphasizing the importance of ambitious goals. Whether personal or professional, the act of envisioning a brighter future is a timeless tradition. We draw parallels between the individual's quest for self-improvement and the collective endeavor to propel coding into a new epoch of innovation.

Introducing ChronoScript: A Tapestry of Time

In the heart of the chapter emerges the concept of ChronoScript, a coding language that transcends the conventional boundaries of time. This unique language acts as a bridge, connecting the past and present, allowing coders to weave a narrative through the annals of time. The syntax of ChronoScript incorporates elements from historical programming languages, creating a tapestry that encompasses the evolution of coding itself.

Chronoscript code

// ChronoScript Syntax Sample

pastCode = "FORTRAN"

presentCode = "Python"

// Concatenating past and present code

chronoCode = pastCode + " -> " + presentCode

// Displaying the narrative through time

print("ChronoScript: " + chronoCode)

This simple ChronoScript snippet concatenates a historical FORTRAN code with a modern Python code, symbolizing the seamless flow of time within the language.

Ambition as the Catalyst for Transformation

The narrative unfolds to emphasize that ambitious goals, when expressed through ChronoScript, become a catalyst for transformation. Whether reimagining outdated systems or pioneering groundbreaking projects, the language serves as a tool for coders to transcend the limitations of the present and create solutions that stand the test of time.

Conclusion: Charting the Course for Tomorrow's Code

As the first chapter concludes, readers are left with a sense of excitement and possibility. The Genesis Code, embodied by ChronoScript, sets the stage for a journey into uncharted territories where coding becomes a dynamic force, shaping not only the future of technology but the narrative of human progress. The call to action resonates: set *ambitious goals, embrace the unique language of ChronoScript, and chart a course for tomorrow's code. The adventure has just begun.*

Chapter 2: "Unravelin

g the Quantum Code"

Introduction:

Quantum Leap into Tomorrow

As the digital realm evolves, a new chapter unfolds—ushering in the era of quantum computing. In this exploration, we delve into the transformative potential of quantum machine learning, poised to be the next technological revolution. The chapter unravels the basic principles of quantum computing, its applications in coding, and introduces a groundbreaking language: "QuantumScript."

Quantum Computing Fundamentals

The narrative kicks off with a primer on quantum computing principles. Quantum bits, or qubits, are introduced, highlighting their unique property of existing in multiple states simultaneously through superposition. Quantum entanglement, the mysterious link between qubits, is explained, paving the way for understanding the immense computational power that quantum systems offer.

Python code

```python
# QuantumScript Sample: Superposition

from quantumscript import Qubit


# Creating a qubit in a superposition state
qubit = Qubit()


# Measuring the qubit state
result = qubit.measure()
```

 # Displaying the result

print("Qubit State: " + result)

This QuantumScript snippet demonstrates the creation of a qubit in a superposition state and measuring its quantum state.

Quantum Machine Learning: A Symbiotic Alliance

The chapter then navigates into the symbiotic relationship between quantum computing and machine learning. The parallel processing capabilities of quantum systems are shown to revolutionize complex problem-solving in machine learning applications. Real-world examples underscore how quantum machine learning algorithms outpace classical counterparts, promising breakthroughs in data analysis, optimization, and pattern recognition.

Python code

 # QuantumScript Sample: Quantum Machine Learning

```python
from quantumscript import QuantumMachineLearning

# Creating a quantum machine learning model
qml_model = QuantumMachineLearning()

# Training the model with quantum data
qml_model.train(quantum_data)

# Making predictions
predictions = qml_model.predict(classical_data)

# Displaying the predictions
print("Quantum Machine Learning Predictions: " + predictions)
```

This QuantumScript snippet illustrates the basic workflow of a quantum machine learning model, showcasing training and prediction phases.

Introducing QuantumScript: Coding in a Parallel Universe

The spotlight then shifts to QuantumScript, a language designed to harness the power of quantum computing. The chapter explores its syntax, showcasing how QuantumScript facilitates parallel processing and quantum operations.

Quantumscript code

// QuantumScript Sample: Quantum Gate Operation

let qubit = Qubit()

// Apply Hadamard gate for superposition

qubit.applyGate(Hadamard)

```
// Entangle qubits
qubit.entangle(anotherQubit)


// Measure the quantum state
let result = qubit.measure()


// Display the result
console.log("Quantum State: " + result)
```

This QuantumScript snippet demonstrates the application of quantum gates and entanglement in a quantum script, reflecting the unique syntax of QuantumScript.

Reshaping the Landscape of Programming

The chapter concludes by envisioning the profound impact of QuantumScript on the programming landscape. It illuminates how quantum computing can disrupt conventional *approaches to problem-solving, cryptography, and optimization. The reader is prompted to envision a future where QuantumScript becomes an integral tool in a coder's arsenal, reshaping the landscape of programming as we know it.*

As we close this chapter, the Quantum Code emerges as a frontier of boundless possibilities, inviting coders to step into a parallel universe where classical limitations dissolve, and the quantum landscape unfolds before them. The call to action echoes: embrace the quantum leap, delve into QuantumScript, and redefine the boundaries of programming in the quantum era. The journey into the unknown has just begun.

Chapter 3: "Deciphering the Unknown"

Introduction: Cracking the Code of Mystery

As we traverse the vast expanse of the coding cosmos, a new frontier beckons—a realm filled with the intrigue of undiscovered coding languages. This chapter embarks on a journey into the unknown, introducing the concept of languages yet to be deciphered by the coding community. Here, the excitement of exploration, the potential for breakthroughs, and the intrinsic link between curiosity and innovation in the world of coding take center stage.

The Tapestry of Known Languages

The chapter begins by acknowledging the rich tapestry of known coding languages that have shaped the evolution of technology. From the foundational languages to the contemporary frameworks, coders have navigated a landscape that continues to expand. Yet, amidst the known, lies the allure of the unknown—a realm where undiscovered languages hold the promise of untold possibilities.

Curiosity as the Catalyst

The narrative then unfolds to celebrate the spirit of curiosity—the driving force that compels coders to venture into uncharted territories. We delve into the psychology of curiosity, exploring how it fuels the desire to uncover the secrets concealed within mysterious coding languages. Real-world examples of historical breakthroughs in coding languages illustrate the transformative power of curiosity as a catalyst for innovation.

Python code

 # Curiosity-Driven Exploration Sample Code

def explore_unknown_language(language):

 # Code to analyze the syntax and structure of the unknown language

...

 # Example of invoking curiosity-driven exploration

explore_unknown_language("MysteryLanguage")

This code snippet symbolizes the essence of curiosity-driven exploration, where coders analyze the syntax and structure of an unknown language.

The Potential Breakthroughs Beyond the Horizon

The narrative shifts to the heart of the chapter—the potential breakthroughs that could emerge from decoding these mysterious languages. We explore the theoretical foundations, computational challenges, and real-world applications that might be unlocked through the understanding of languages yet to be discovered. The chapter paints a picture of a future where the deciphering of unknown languages could lead to innovations that reshape the coding landscape.

Innovation: The Art of Decoding

The spotlight then turns to the symbiotic relationship between curiosity and innovation. We delve into how the act of decoding unknown languages fosters innovative thinking. Case studies highlight instances where decoding mysterious languages has paved the way for groundbreaking solutions, emphasizing the importance of thinking beyond the established norms in the world of coding.

Python code

Innovative Decoding Sample Code

def innovative_decoding(language):

 # Code to experiment and innovate with the decoded language

...

 # Example of invoking innovative decoding

innovative_decoding("InnovativeLanguage")

This code snippet encapsulates the idea of experimenting and innovating with a decoded language, showcasing the creative process.

Conclusion: A Call to the Curious Minds

As the chapter concludes, readers are left with a call to action—a call to embrace curiosity as a guiding light in the coding journey. The unknown languages become an invitation for coders to be pioneers, to decode the secrets hidden within lines of code yet to be understood. The chapter stands as a testament to the infinite possibilities that *curiosity and innovation hold in the world of coding—an ever-expanding universe where the curious mind is the compass guiding us into the unknown. The exploration of undiscovered languages becomes not just a venture into the code but a journey into the limitless realms of human ingenuity.*

Chapter 4:

"Brightening the Present"

Introduction: Code

for Change

In this chapter, we shift our gaze to the present, exploring the impactful role that coding plays in addressing contemporary challenges. We delve into real-world examples where technology, driven by code, has become a catalyst for positive change. From environmental sustainability to social justice, we unravel the ways in which coding contributes to creating a brighter and more sustainable present.

Coding for Environmental Stewardship

The narrative begins with a focus on the environmental challenges our world faces.

Real-world projects exemplify how coding is employed to monitor, mitigate, and raise awareness about issues such as climate change and conservation efforts. The chapter illustrates how the skills acquired through learning future coding languages can be applied to create innovative solutions for a more sustainable and eco-friendly world.

Python code

 # Environmental Monitoring Sample Code

def monitor_environment(sensor_data):

 # Code to analyze and process environmental sensor data

...

 # Example of environmental monitoring in action

sensor_data = get_sensor_data()

monitor_environment(sensor_data)

This code snippet symbolizes the process of coding for environmental monitoring, analyzing and processing data to address ecological challenges.

Coding for Social Justice and Equality

The narrative then shifts its focus to social justice, showcasing instances where coding has been harnessed to address issues of inequality. Real-world examples highlight how technology and coding contribute to providing equal access to education, healthcare, and social services. The chapter emphasizes the role of coding skills in crafting solutions that empower marginalized communities.

Python code

 # Social Justice Application Sample Code

def provide_social_services(user_data):

 # Code to implement a system for providing social services

...

 # Example of a social justice application in action

user_data = get_user_data()

provide_social_services(user_data)

This code snippet represents the development of a system that utilizes coding to provide social services, contributing to the promotion of social justice.

Coding for Humanitarian Causes

The narrative widens its scope to encompass humanitarian efforts where coding becomes a crucial tool in crisis response and global health initiatives. Real-world applications demonstrate how coding skills are applied to enhance disaster response, support refugees, and combat global health crises. The chapter explores how learning future coding languages can equip individuals to contribute meaningfully to humanitarian causes.

Python code

Humanitarian Coding Sample Code

def disaster_response(affected_area):

Code to coordinate disaster response efforts

...

Example of humanitarian coding in action

affected_area = get_affected_area()

disaster_response(affected_area)

This code snippet exemplifies the role of coding in coordinating disaster response efforts, showcasing the practical application of coding skills in humanitarian endeavors.

Conclusion: The Power of Code in the Present Moment

As the chapter draws to a close, readers are immersed in a world where coding is not just a technical skill but a force for positive change in the present. The call to action resonates—to leverage coding skills for creating solutions that address the pressing challenges of our time. The skills acquired through learning future coding languages become not just tools for tomorrow but instruments for crafting a brighter and more sustainable present. The chapter stands as a testament to the transformative power of code in shaping a world that reflects our collective commitment to environmental stewardship, social justice, and humanitarian values. The journey continues, with each line of code contributing to a more vibrant and equitable present.

Chapter 5: "The Theory of

Universe in Code"

Introduction: Code and

Cosmos Entwined

In this concluding chapter, we embark on a cosmic journey that intertwines the fabric of coding with the grand theory of the universe. As we explore the parallels between the structure of the cosmos and the logic of coding languages, the chapter proposes a tantalizing idea—that the universe itself may be an intricate code waiting to be deciphered. The call to action resonates with readers to continue their exploration of the limitless possibilities of coding, understanding the universe through the lens of ChronoScript, QuantumScript, and the languages yet to be discovered.

The Elegant Harmony of Code and Cosmos

The chapter begins by drawing parallels between the elegant structures of coding languages and the cosmic order of the universe. It delves into the notion that, much like the syntax that governs a programming language, the laws of physics and the mathematical principles underlying the cosmos may follow an intricately structured code.

Python code

 # Cosmic Harmony Sample Code

def simulate_cosmic_phenomenon():

 # Code to simulate a cosmic phenomenon using mathematical principles

...

 # Example of simulating a cosmic phenomenon through coding

simulate_cosmic_phenomenon()

This code snippet represents the idea of simulating cosmic phenomena through the application of mathematical principles, showcasing the harmony between code and cosmos.

Decoding the Cosmic Script

The narrative unfolds to explore the provocative idea that the universe itself may be a vast cosmic script waiting to be deciphered. Drawing inspiration from ChronoScript and QuantumScript, the chapter encourages readers to contemplate the possibility of unraveling the mysteries of the cosmos through the application of advanced coding languages.

Python code

```python
# Deciphering the Cosmic Code Sample Code

def decipher_cosmic_script():
```

Code to decipher the cosmic script,
revealing the mysteries of the universe

...

Example of invoking the deciphering of the
cosmic code

decipher_cosmic_script()

This code snippet symbolizes the concept of deciphering the cosmic script through the application of coding, a metaphor for understanding the mysteries of the universe.

The Universe as a Quantum Codebase

The chapter takes an intriguing turn by proposing the idea of the universe as a vast quantum codebase. It explores the theoretical framework that considers the universe as a quantum computer, where the fundamental operations driving cosmic phenomena are akin to the computations executed in a quantum system.

Quantumscript code

// QuantumScript Universe Simulation Sample Code

let cosmic_qubits = initialize_cosmic_qubits()

// Apply quantum operations to simulate cosmic phenomena

cosmic_qubits.applyOperations()

// Measure the quantum state of the cosmic codebase

let cosmic_state = cosmic_qubits.measure()

// Display the result

console.log("Cosmic Codebase State: " + cosmic_state)

This QuantumScript snippet represents a hypothetical simulation of the universe as a quantum codebase, showcasing the integration of quantum operations to simulate cosmic phenomena.

A Call to Explore: Beyond the Known and Unknown

As the chapter draws to a close, readers are left with a resounding call to action—an invitation to continue exploring the limitless possibilities that coding offers in understanding the universe. Whether through the lens of ChronoScript, QuantumScript, or languages yet to be discovered, the journey is one of perpetual curiosity and exploration. The code becomes not just a tool but a medium through which the mysteries of the cosmos are unveiled.

Epilogue: Beyond the Coding Cosmos

The final pages of the chapter serve as an epilogue to the entire book. The reader is reminded that the exploration of the coding cosmos is an ongoing quest, with the universe itself as a canvas waiting to be painted with the strokes of code. The call to action echoes—continue to code, continue to explore, and continue to unravel the cosmic mysteries that beckon to the curious minds of coders. As the book concludes, the reader is encouraged to carry the spirit of exploration and understanding into their coding endeavors, inspired by the vastness of the coding cosmos and the boundless possibilities that lie beyond. The journey continues, and the universe, in all its complexity, awaits the next lines of code to be written.

Summary

:

In "Coding Cosmos," readers embark on a transformative journey through the realms of coding, exploring the past, present, and future of programming languages. The book unfolds across five chapters, each offering a unique perspective on the intersection of coding with time, quantum computing, undiscovered languages, present challenges, and the cosmic mysteries that might be encoded in the fabric of the universe.

Chapter 1: "The Genesis Code" The journey commences with an exploration of the concept of New Year resolutions in the context of coding the future. The chapter introduces the unique *coding language, "ChronoScript," which concatenates the past and present worlds, enabling coders to weave a narrative through time. The significance of setting ambitious goals and the transformative power of ChronoScript lay the foundation for the book's exploration.*

In code snippets, the syntax of ChronoScript is symbolized, emphasizing the language's ability to blend historical coding languages with modern ones. The reader is encouraged to embrace ambitious goals and leverage ChronoScript as a tool for personal and professional transformation.

Chapter 2: "Unraveling the Quantum Code"

The narrative then shifts to the cutting-edge world of quantum computing, positioning quantum machine learning as the next technological revolution. Basic principles of quantum computing, such as superposition and entanglement, are demystified. The concept of a new quantum coding language, "QuantumScript," is introduced, promising to reshape the landscape of programming.

QuantumScript is brought to life through code snippets, illustrating its syntax and the application of quantum principles. The chapter underscores the symbiotic alliance between quantum computing and machine learning, showcasing the transformative potential of QuantumScript in solving complex problems.

Chapter 3: "Deciphering the Unknown" The exploration takes a daring turn into the unknown, introducing the notion of undiscovered coding languages that are yet to be deciphered by the coding community. The chapter celebrates the excitement of exploring uncharted territories and delves into the potential breakthroughs that could emerge from decoding these mysterious languages. The importance of curiosity and innovation in the coding world is highlighted.

Code snippets capture the essence of curiosity-driven exploration and innovative decoding, portraying the process of analyzing and experimenting with unknown languages. The chapter concludes with a call to embrace the *mysteries of undiscovered languages, recognizing them as essential elements in the ever-evolving world of coding.*

Chapter 4: "Brightening the Present" *Shifting focus to the present, this chapter explores how coding contributes to making a positive impact on current challenges. Real-world examples demonstrate the application of technology and coding in addressing environmental issues, social justice, and humanitarian causes. The skills acquired through learning future coding languages are showcased as tools for creating a brighter and more sustainable present.*

Code snippets symbolize the coding applications in environmental monitoring, social justice initiatives, and humanitarian efforts. The chapter concludes with a call to action, urging readers to leverage coding skills for positive change and contribute to a more vibrant and equitable present.

Chapter 5: "The Theory of Universe in Code" *The final chapter elevates the narrative, connecting coding with the grand theory of the* universe. Parallels between the structure of the cosmos and the logic of coding languages are explored, entertaining the idea that the universe itself may be a vast, intricate code awaiting decipherment. The chapter concludes with a call to action for readers to continue exploring the limitless possibilities of coding and understanding the universe through the lens of ChronoScript, QuantumScript, and the languages yet to be discovered.

Code snippets depict the simulation of cosmic phenomena, the deciphering of the cosmic code, and the hypothetical application of QuantumScript in understanding the universe as a quantum codebase. The reader is left with a profound sense of awe and inspiration, recognizing the interconnectedness of code and the cosmos.

Epilogue: Beyond the Coding Cosmos The book concludes with an epilogue, reminding readers that the exploration of the coding cosmos is an ongoing journey. It is an invitation to carry the spirit of exploration and *understanding into their coding endeavors, inspired by the vastness of the coding cosmos and the boundless possibilities that lie beyond. The journey continues, and the universe, in all its complexity, awaits the next lines of code to be written.*

Glossary:

1. **ChronoScript:** *A unique coding language introduced in Chapter 1 that concatenates the past and present coding worlds, allowing programmers to weave a narrative through time.*

2. **QuantumScript:** *A hypothetical coding language introduced in Chapter 2,*

designed to harness the power of quantum computing and reshape the programming landscape.

3. **Qubit:** *The fundamental unit of quantum information in quantum computing, capable of existing in multiple states simultaneously through superposition.*

4. **Superposition:** *A principle in quantum mechanics that allows quantum systems, such as qubits, to exist in multiple states at the same time.*

5. **Entanglement:** *A phenomenon in quantum physics where two or more qubits become correlated and share information, influencing each other's states.*

6. **Quantum Machine Learning:** *The fusion of quantum computing principles with machine learning, explored in Chapter 2 as a potential technological revolution.*

7. **Curiosity-Driven Exploration:** *The approach discussed in Chapter 3,*

emphasizing the importance of curiosity as a catalyst for exploring undiscovered coding languages.

8. **Innovative Decoding:** *The concept introduced in Chapter 3, focusing on experimenting and innovating with decoded unknown coding languages.*

9. **Environmental Monitoring:** *A real-world application of coding discussed in Chapter 4, involving the use of technology to monitor and address environmental issues.*

10. **Social Justice Application:** *A coding application highlighted in Chapter 4, demonstrating how technology and coding can contribute to social justice and equality.*

11. **Humanitarian Coding:** *The use of coding in humanitarian efforts, explored in Chapter 4, such as disaster response and global health initiatives.*

12. **Cosmic Harmony:** *A metaphorical concept in Chapter 5, illustrating the*

parallels between the structure of coding languages and the order of the cosmos.

13.	**Deciphering the Cosmic Code:** *The theoretical idea presented in Chapter 5 that the universe itself may be a vast code awaiting decipherment.*

14.	**Cosmic Script:** *A speculative concept discussed in Chapter 5, suggesting that the universe operates according to a script, possibly encoded in the laws of physics.*

15.	**Cosmic Qubits:** *The hypothetical quantum units introduced in Chapter 5, representing the idea of the universe as a quantum codebase.*

16.	**Coding Cosmos:** *The overarching theme of the book, emphasizing the interconnectedness of coding principles with various aspects of the universe.*

17.	**Ambitious Goals:** *The concept discussed in Chapter 1, stressing the importance of setting ambitious goals for personal and professional transformation.*

18. **Coding Revolution:** *A recurring theme throughout the book, referring to the transformative impact of new coding languages and technologies.*

19. **Symbiotic Alliance:** *Highlighted in Chapter 2, indicating the mutually beneficial relationship between quantum computing and machine learning.*

20. **Undiscovered Languages:** *Discussed in Chapter 3, referring to coding languages that have not yet been deciphered or explored by the coding community.*

21. **Positive Impact:** *Emphasized in Chapter 4, referring to the beneficial influence of coding on addressing real-world challenges and making a positive difference.*

22. **Present Challenges:** *The focus of Chapter 4, exploring how coding can contribute to solving current issues,*

including environmental concerns and social justice.

23.   **Limitless Possibilities:** *A recurring theme throughout the book, encouraging readers to explore the vast and boundless potential within the coding cosmos.*

24.   **Future-Proof Coding:** *Emphasized in Chapter 4, indicating coding practices and languages that remain relevant and effective in the face of future challenges.*

25.   **Boundless Exploration:** *Encouraged in the Epilogue, urging readers to continue exploring and pushing the boundaries of coding knowledge and understanding.*

26.   **Interconnectedness:** *A key concept in the Epilogue, highlighting the interconnected nature of code and the universe, suggesting that coding principles mirror cosmic order.*

27.   **Awe and Inspiration:** *Emotions evoked in the reader by the exploration of*

the coding cosmos, especially in the concluding chapters.

28.   **Quantum Leap:** *A metaphorical concept in Chapter 2, symbolizing a significant advancement or transformation in the world of coding, particularly with the advent of quantum computing.*

29.   **Intricate Code:** *Describing the potential coding nature of the universe, introduced in Chapter 5 as a speculative idea.*

30.   **Simulation of Cosmic Phenomena:** *Introduced in Chapter 5, depicting the hypothetical use of coding to simulate and understand cosmic events.*

This glossary provides a snapshot of key terms and concepts found in "Coding Cosmos," capturing the essence of the book's exploration into the intersection of coding and the broader cosmos.

Here are 101 possible

New Year resolutions:

1. Cultivate a daily gratitude practice.

2. Learn a new instrument.

3. Read a book from a genre you wouldn't typically explore.

4. Start a mindfulness meditation routine.

5. Volunteer for a cause you're passionate about.

6. *Explore a new hobby, like painting or photography.*

7. *Adopt a plant-based diet for a day each week.*

8. *Practice random acts of kindness.*

9. *Join a local club or group to meet new people.*

10. *Take a social media detox.*

11. *Write a letter to a friend or family member each month.*

12. *Organize a neighborhood cleanup day.*

13. *Start a journal to document your thoughts and experiences.*

14. *Learn a new language.*

15. *Try a new workout routine or exercise class.*

16. *Start a DIY home improvement project.*

17.	Cut down on single-use plastics.

18.	Attend a live performance, whether it's theater, music, or dance.

19.	Take a cooking class to learn new recipes.

20.	Foster or adopt a pet from a local shelter.

21.	Learn to code or improve your coding skills.

22.	Begin a regular walking routine.

23.	Establish a consistent sleep schedule.

24.	Cultivate a minimalist lifestyle.

25.	Practice saying 'no' when necessary for your well-being.

26.	Engage in a monthly self-care day.

27.	Take up cycling as a form of exercise.

28.	Try a new type of cuisine each month.

29. Develop a budget and stick to it.

30. Volunteer at a local community garden.

31. Learn to play chess or improve your chess skills.

32. Attend a workshop or seminar to enhance your professional skills.

33. Dedicate time each week for creative expression, whether through art, writing, or music.

34. Practice deep-breathing exercises regularly.

35. Commit to a daily stretching routine.

36. Invest time in learning about a historical period or event.

37. Foster a more sustainable lifestyle by reducing waste.

38. Attend a local lecture or discussion on a topic outside your comfort zone.

39.	Join a recreational sports league.

40.	Limit screen time and prioritize face-to-face interactions.

41.	Start a DIY home garden.

42.	Practice active listening in conversations.

43.	Experiment with a new hairstyle or wardrobe.

44.	Learn to juggle or master a new party trick.

45.	Explore different types of teas or coffees.

46.	Practice a musical instrument regularly.

47.	Take a class in photography or videography.

48.	Commit to regular dental check-ups and oral hygiene.

49.	*Build a capsule wardrobe to simplify your clothing choices.*

50.	*Establish a routine for regular self-reflection.*

51.	*Try your hand at poetry or creative writing.*

52.	*Dedicate time for stargazing or learning about astronomy.*

53.	*Learn to sew or mend your clothes.*

54.	*Practice a digital detox one day a week.*

55.	*Commit to sending handwritten notes for special occasions.*

56.	*Learn about a new culture through its literature, cuisine, and traditions.*

57.	*Dedicate time each week for personal development.*

58.	*Participate in a community service project.*

59.   Explore different forms of dance, from salsa to hip-hop.

60.   Contribute to a crowdfunding campaign for a cause you believe in.

61.   Start a blog or a vlog to document your experiences and thoughts.

62.   Create a vision board for your aspirations.

63.   Establish a routine for unplanned adventures or spontaneous outings.

64.   Learn about and practice mindfulness techniques.

65.   Set boundaries for work-life balance.

66.   Practice positive self-talk.

67.   Develop a skincare routine for healthier skin.

68.   Commit to reducing energy consumption in your home.

69.   *Explore different types of meditation practices.*

70.   *Take up bird watching or nature photography.*

71.   *Set aside time for regular digital decluttering.*

72.   *Commit to reading a news article from a reputable source daily.*

73.   *Attend a local farmers' market regularly.*

74.   *Practice the art of active gratitude.*

75.   *Learn to perform basic car maintenance tasks.*

76.   *Commit to supporting local businesses.*

77.   *Attend a community event or festival.*

78.   *Learn basic first aid skills.*

79.   *Experiment with a new hairstyle or hair color.*

80.   Practice positive affirmations.

81.   Explore different types of cheeses or wines.

82.   Commit to using public transportation or carpooling.

83.   Dedicate time for DIY crafting projects.

84.   Start a book club with friends or join an existing one.

85.   Learn about the history and culture of a country you're less familiar with.

86.   Commit to reducing single-use plastic in your daily life.

87.   Take up fishing or try a new outdoor activity.

88.   Develop a habit of taking regular breaks at work.

89.   Attend a local workshop on a topic of interest.

90.   Set aside time for regular digital detox weekends.

91.   Commit to reducing your carbon footprint.

92.   Learn about different types of teas and their health benefits.

93.   Dedicate time for regular hiking or nature walks.

94.   Explore the world of podcasts on various topics.

95.   Practice intentional breathing exercises.

96.   Learn the basics of coding or programming.

97.   Commit to reducing food waste in your household.

98.   Take up a DIY home decor project.

99.   Establish a routine for practicing mindfulness in nature.

100.   Attend a cultural event or performance from a different heritage.

101.   Explore different types of art, from painting to sculpture.

Develop Logic Building Attitude

Building a logical thinking attitude involves breaking down problems into smaller, more manageable parts, identifying patterns, and understanding relationships between different elements. Here's a simple example to illustrate logic building using a Python code:

Problem Statement:

Write a program that takes a list of numbers and returns the sum of all even numbers in the list.

Logic Building Steps:

Understand the Problem:

What is the input? A list of numbers.

What is the output? The sum of even numbers in the list.

Break It Down:

Iterate through each number in the list.

Check if the number is even.

If it's even, add it to the sum.

Identify Patterns:

Even numbers are divisible by 2.

Understand Relationships:

The sum is built by adding each even number.

Develop the Logic:

Initialize a variable to store the sum.

Iterate through each number in the list.

Check if the number is even using the modulo operator (%).

If it's even, add it to the sum.

Now, let's translate this logic into Python code:

Python code

```python
def sum_of_even_numbers(numbers):
    # Initialize sum to 0
    even_sum = 0

    # Iterate through each number in the list
    for number in numbers:
        # Check if the number is even
        if number % 2 == 0:
            # If it's even, add it to the sum
            even_sum += number

    # Return the sum of even numbers
    return even_sum


# Example Usage
numbers_list = [1, 2, 3, 4, 5, 6, 7, 8, 9, 10]
result = sum_of_even_numbers(numbers_list)
print("Sum of even numbers:", result)
```

In this example, the sum_of_even_numbers function takes a list of numbers, iterates through each number, checks if it's even, and accumulates the sum. The result is then printed.

This simple problem demonstrates the process of logic building: understanding the problem, breaking it down, identifying patterns, understanding relationships, and finally, translating the logic into code. Developing a logical thinking attitude involves practicing these steps with more complex problems over time.

Additional Example:

Finding the Average of Positive Numbers

Problem Statement:

Write a program that takes a list of numbers and returns the average of all positive numbers in the list.

Logic Building Steps:

Understand the Problem:

What is the input? A list of numbers.

What is the output? The average of positive numbers in the list.

Break It Down:

Initialize variables for the sum and count of positive numbers.

Iterate through each number in the list.

Check if the number is positive.

If it's positive, add it to the sum and increment the count.

Identify Patterns:

Positive numbers are greater than 0.

Understand Relationships:

The average is calculated by dividing the sum of positive numbers by their count.

Develop the Logic:

Initialize variables: sum_positive, count_positive to 0.

Iterate through each number in the list.

Check if the number is positive (greater than 0).

If positive, add it to sum_positive and increment count_positive.

Calculate average as sum_positive divided by count_positive.

Now, let's translate this logic into Python code:

Python code

```python
def average_of_positive_numbers(numbers):
    # Initialize variables
    sum_positive = 0
    count_positive = 0


    # Iterate through each number in the list
    for number in numbers:
        # Check if the number is positive
        if number > 0:
            # If positive, add it to sum_positive and
            increment count_positive
            sum_positive += number
            count_positive += 1


    # Avoid division by zero
    if count_positive == 0:
        return 0  # Return 0 if no positive
        numbers are found
```

```python
    # Calculate average
    average = sum_positive / count_positive

    # Return the average of positive numbers
    return average

# Example Usage
numbers_list = [5, -2, 10, -8, 3, 0, 7]
result = average_of_positive_numbers(numbers_list)
print("Average of positive numbers:", result)
```

This example demonstrates the process of building logic to find the average of positive numbers in a list. It involves initializing variables, iterating through the list, checking conditions, and performing calculations.

Summary of Logic Building Code:

Problem Understanding:

Clearly define the problem and understand the input/output requirements.

Break It Down:

Divide the problem into smaller, manageable tasks.

Identify Patterns:

Recognize recurring themes or conditions in the problem.

Understand Relationships:

Grasp how different elements or variables relate to each other.

Develop the Logic:

Build the step-by-step logic to solve the problem, considering conditions, loops, and calculations.

Applying these steps consistently develops a logical thinking attitude. Practice with a variety of problems to enhance your problem-solving skills and adapt the logic building process to more complex scenarios.

New Year

problem

solving

attitude

how to

develop:

Developing a problem-solving attitude is a valuable skill that can enhance various aspects of your life. Here are some practical steps to cultivate a New Year problem-solving attitude:

Embrace a Growth Mindset:

Adopt the belief that your abilities and intelligence can be developed through dedication and hard work.

See challenges as opportunities for learning and growth rather than obstacles.

Define Clear Goals:

Clearly define your goals for the year. Having a clear direction helps you identify and solve problems that align with your objectives.

Break Down Big Goals:

Divide larger goals into smaller, more manageable tasks. This makes it easier to tackle challenges step by step.

Prioritize and Organize:

Prioritize tasks based on their importance and urgency.

Organize your time and resources efficiently to address each task effectively.

Develop Critical Thinking Skills:

Analyze situations objectively and consider multiple perspectives.

Evaluate the information available before making decisions.

Be Adaptable:

Embrace change and be open to adapting your strategies when needed.

View unexpected situations as opportunities to demonstrate flexibility and resilience.

Learn from Mistakes:

See mistakes as part of the learning process.

Analyze what went wrong, identify areas for improvement, and use this knowledge to refine your approach.

Seek Feedback:

Actively seek feedback from peers, mentors, or experts.

Constructive feedback provides valuable insights and alternative perspectives.

Enhance Communication Skills:

Clearly articulate your thoughts and ideas.

Listen actively to others' perspectives and collaborate effectively.

Build a Network:

Connect with individuals who possess diverse skills and experiences.

A diverse network can provide different viewpoints and solutions to problems.

Continuous Learning:

Stay curious and commit to continuous learning.

Acquire new skills and stay updated on industry trends and developments.

Practice Mindfulness:

Practice mindfulness techniques to stay focused and calm during challenging situations.

A clear mind facilitates better problem-solving.

Use Problem-Solving Models:

Familiarize yourself with problem-solving models such as the "IDEAL" model (Identify the problem, Define the context, Explore *potential solutions, Act on the best solution, Look back and learn).*

Celebrate Small Wins:

Acknowledge and celebrate your achievements, no matter how small.

Positive reinforcement encourages a problem-solving mindset.

Set Realistic Expectations:

Be realistic about what you can achieve.

Setting achievable goals prevents overwhelm and fosters a positive problem-solving approach.

Seek Professional Development Opportunities:

Attend workshops, seminars, or courses relevant to your field.

Investing in your professional development enhances problem-solving skills.

Encourage Creativity:

Cultivate creativity to generate innovative solutions.

Allow yourself to think outside the box when faced with challenges.

Stay Positive:

Maintain a positive attitude even in challenging situations.

Positivity fosters resilience and perseverance.

Create a Problem-Solving Routine:

Establish a routine that includes regular problem-solving exercises.

Consistency reinforces a proactive problem-solving mindset.

Reflect Regularly:

Take time to reflect on your problem-solving experiences.

Consider what worked well and what could be improved.

By incorporating these steps into your daily life, you can cultivate a problem-solving attitude that will empower you to tackle challenges effectively and navigate the uncertainties of the coming year with confidence.

How to deal with procrastination

Dealing with procrastination involves adopting strategies to overcome the tendency to delay or postpone tasks. Here are practical steps to help you overcome procrastination:

Understand the Root Cause:

Identify the reasons behind your procrastination. It could be fear of failure, lack of motivation, or feeling overwhelmed.

Break Tasks into Smaller Steps:

Divide larger tasks into smaller, more manageable steps. This makes the overall task less intimidating and more achievable.

Set Clear Goals:

Clearly define your goals and establish a timeline. Knowing what you need to achieve and when can provide a sense of direction and urgency.

Prioritize Tasks:

Prioritize tasks based on their importance and deadlines. Focus on high-priority items first to avoid feeling overwhelmed.

Use the Pomodoro Technique:

Break your work into intervals, traditionally 25 minutes of focused work followed by a 5-minute break. This can help maintain focus and reduce the pressure of a looming task.

Eliminate Distractions:

Identify and minimize potential distractions. Turn off notifications, create a dedicated workspace, and communicate your need for focused time to those around you.

Set Specific Deadlines:

Establish specific deadlines for tasks, even if they are self-imposed. Having a sense of urgency can counteract procrastination.

Visualize Success:

Imagine the positive outcomes and benefits of completing the task. Visualization can motivate you to start working.

Start with the Easiest Task:

Begin your work with the easiest or most enjoyable task on your list. This can build momentum and make it easier to transition to more challenging tasks.

Use a To-Do List:

Create a to-do list with clear, actionable items. Crossing off completed tasks can provide a sense of accomplishment.

Reward Yourself:

Establish a system of rewards for completing tasks. Treat yourself to something enjoyable after completing a challenging task.

Seek Accountability:

Share your goals and deadlines with someone who can hold you accountable. Knowing that others are aware of your commitments can increase motivation.

Change Your Environment:

If you're stuck in a procrastination loop, change your environment. A new setting can bring a fresh perspective and break the cycle.

Address Perfectionism:

Understand that perfectionism can contribute to procrastination. Focus on progress rather than waiting for perfection.

Use Implementation Intentions:

Clearly state when, where, and how you will complete a task. This helps create a mental plan and increases the likelihood of follow-through.

Consider the Consequences:

Reflect on the consequences of not completing the task. Understanding the negative impact of procrastination can be a powerful motivator.

Practice Self-Compassion:

Be kind to yourself. Understand that everyone procrastinates at times, and it's okay. Focus on progress rather than self-criticism.

Break the Task into Timed Segments:

Set a timer for a specific amount of time (e.g., 15 minutes) and commit to working on the task until the timer goes off. This makes the task feel more manageable.

Cultivate a Growth Mindset:

Embrace challenges as opportunities for growth. A growth mindset can shift your perspective on tasks from threatening to empowering.

Seek Professional Help if Needed:

If procrastination is significantly affecting your life, consider seeking the help of a counselor or therapist to address underlying issues.

Remember that overcoming procrastination is a gradual process, and finding the strategies that work best for you may require some experimentation. Consistency and self-compassion are key elements in developing effective habits and minimizing procrastination.

How to resolve

screen time

Resolving screen time issues involves creating a healthy balance between the use of digital devices and other aspects of life. Here are some practical steps to manage and reduce screen time:

Set Clear Limits:

Establish specific daily or weekly limits for screen time. Clearly communicate these limits to yourself and others in your household.

Create a Schedule:

Develop a structured daily or weekly schedule that includes dedicated time for work, socializing, physical activity, and relaxation without screens.

Use Screen Time Tracking Apps:

Utilize apps or built-in features on devices that track your screen time. Reviewing this data can help you become more aware of your usage patterns.

Establish Tech-Free Zones:

Designate specific areas in your home where the use of electronic devices is not allowed. This could include the bedroom during sleep hours or the dining table during meals.

Prioritize Offline Activities:

Engage in offline activities such as reading, exercising, or pursuing hobbies that do not involve screens. This helps diversify your interests and reduces dependency on digital devices.

Set Boundaries for Social Media:

Allocate specific time slots for checking and responding to social media. Avoid mindless scrolling by setting a timer for your social media use.

Introduce Screen-Free Activities:

Plan activities that do not involve screens, such as board games, outdoor activities, or face-to-face interactions with friends and family.

Practice the 20-20-20 Rule:

Follow the 20-20-20 rule to reduce eye strain. Every 20 minutes, look at something 20 feet away for at least 20 seconds.

Establish Screen-Free Times:

Designate specific times of the day or week as screen-free. This could be during meals, before bedtime, or a certain period during the weekend.

Encourage Physical Activity:

Incorporate regular physical activity into your routine. Exercise not only promotes well-being but also reduces the time available for excessive screen use.

Explore Offline Hobbies:

Discover and engage in hobbies that do not involve screens, such as painting, gardening, or playing a musical instrument.

Educate Yourself on Screen Time Effects:

Learn about the potential negative effects of excessive screen time on physical and mental health. Understanding the risks can motivate behavior change.

Model Healthy Behavior:

Demonstrate healthy screen time habits to those around you, especially if you have children. Set an example by balancing your own screen use.

Use Technology Wisely:

When using screens, choose activities that add value to your life, such as educational content, skill-building apps, or connecting with loved ones.

Practice Mindful Screen Use:

Be intentional about your screen time. Avoid multitasking and focus on one task at a time. Mindful use can enhance the quality of your digital interactions.

Create a Tech-Free Night Routine:

Establish a tech-free routine before bedtime. This helps improve sleep quality by reducing exposure to the stimulating effects of screens.

Involve Others:

Discuss screen time boundaries with family members or roommates. Collaboratively set guidelines to create a supportive environment.

Plan Outdoor Activities:

Spend time outdoors regularly. Whether it's a walk in the park or a weekend hike, outdoor activities provide a healthy alternative to screen-based entertainment.

Evaluate and Adjust:

Regularly assess your screen time habits. If you notice patterns of excessive use, reevaluate and adjust your limits and strategies accordingly.

Consider Professional Help:

If you find it challenging to manage screen time on your own, consider seeking guidance from a mental health professional or a technology addiction specialist.

Remember that achieving a healthy balance with screen time is a gradual process. Start with small, manageable changes and adjust your approach based on what works best for you. The goal is to create a sustainable and mindful relationship with digital devices.

How one can be fit and fine and live a healthy life:

Maintaining a fit and healthy lifestyle involves a holistic approach that encompasses physical activity, balanced nutrition, mental well-being, and healthy habits. Here are some practical tips to help you live a healthy life:

Regular Exercise:

Engage in regular physical activity. Aim for at least 150 minutes of moderate-intensity exercise or 75 minutes of vigorous-intensity exercise per week.

Include a mix of aerobic exercises (like walking, running, or cycling), strength training, and flexibility exercises.

Balanced Nutrition:

Consume a well-balanced diet rich in fruits, vegetables, whole grains, lean proteins, and healthy fats.

Stay hydrated by drinking an adequate amount of water throughout the day.

Adequate Sleep:

Prioritize getting 7-9 hours of quality sleep each night. Develop a consistent sleep routine to improve sleep quality.

Stress Management:

Practice stress-reducing techniques such as meditation, deep breathing, yoga, or mindfulness.

Establish boundaries to manage stressors effectively.

Regular Health Check-ups:

Schedule regular health check-ups and screenings to monitor your health status and address potential issues early on.

Limit Processed Foods and Sugars:

Minimize the intake of processed foods, sugary beverages, and excessive amounts of added sugars.

Opt for whole, nutrient-dense foods to support your overall health.

Stay Hydrated:

Drink an adequate amount of water daily. Water plays a crucial role in various bodily functions, including digestion and temperature regulation.

Limit Alcohol and Tobacco:

Consume alcohol in moderation, if at all. Avoid smoking and exposure to secondhand smoke.

Maintain a Healthy Weight:

Strive for a healthy weight based on your body type and height. Focus on overall well-being rather than unrealistic body image standards.

Build Strong Social Connections:

Cultivate and maintain healthy relationships with friends and family.

Social connections contribute to emotional well-being and provide a support system.

Practice Mindful Eating:

Eat with awareness, paying attention to hunger and fullness cues.

Avoid distractions, such as watching TV or using electronic devices, while eating.

Limit Screen Time:

Manage screen time, especially before bedtime. Excessive screen use can impact sleep quality.

Follow the 20-20-20 rule to reduce eye strain: every 20 minutes, look at something 20 feet away for at least 20 seconds.

Incorporate Leisure Activities:

Engage in hobbies and activities you enjoy. This contributes to mental and emotional well-being.

Hygiene Practices:

Follow good hygiene practices, including regular handwashing, oral care, and personal hygiene.

Maintain a clean and healthy living environment.

Educate Yourself:

Stay informed about health-related topics. Understand the nutritional value of foods and the benefits of regular exercise.

Set Realistic Goals:

Set achievable health and fitness goals. Break larger goals into smaller, manageable steps to maintain motivation.

Limit Caffeine Intake:

Moderate your caffeine consumption, especially later in the day, to support better sleep.

Cultivate a Positive Mindset:

Foster a positive attitude and practice self-compassion.

Celebrate your achievements, no matter how small, and learn from setbacks.

Environmental Wellness:

Be mindful of your surroundings. Surround yourself with positive influences and create a healthy living environment.

Continuous Learning:

Stay curious and open to learning. Adapt and incorporate new health-related information into your lifestyle.

Remember, living a healthy life is a journey, not a destination. Small, consistent changes over time contribute significantly to your overall well-being. Consult with healthcare professionals or certified experts when needed to tailor health recommendations to your individual needs.

How to be prepared with future diseases and give

possible solution:

Being prepared for future diseases involves a proactive approach to health that includes preventive measures, staying informed, and adopting healthy lifestyle practices. Here are some guidelines to help you prepare for potential health challenges and diseases:

1. Stay Informed:

Keep yourself updated on current health trends, emerging diseases, and advancements in medical research.

Follow reputable health organizations, read scientific publications, and stay informed about global health issues.

2. Adopt a Healthy Lifestyle:

Balanced Nutrition: Consume a nutritious, well-balanced diet rich in fruits, vegetables, whole grains, lean proteins, and healthy fats.

Regular Exercise: Engage in regular physical activity to maintain overall health and boost your immune system.

Adequate Sleep: Prioritize sufficient and quality sleep to support immune function and overall well-being.

Stress Management: Practice stress-reducing techniques such as meditation, deep breathing, or mindfulness.

3. Practice Preventive Healthcare:

Schedule regular check-ups and screenings with healthcare professionals to detect potential health issues early on.

Follow recommended vaccination schedules to protect against preventable diseases.

4. Maintain a Healthy Weight:

Achieve and maintain a healthy weight through a combination of balanced nutrition and regular exercise.

Consult with healthcare professionals for personalized advice on weight management.

5. Practice Good Hygiene:

Follow proper hygiene practices, including regular handwashing, to reduce the risk of infections.

Be mindful of personal and environmental cleanliness.

6. Limit Harmful Habits:

Avoid tobacco and limit alcohol consumption to promote overall health.

Minimize exposure to environmental pollutants and toxins.

7. Build a Supportive Social Network:

Cultivate strong social connections to support your mental and emotional well-being.

Share health-related information with friends and family to collectively adopt healthy practices.

---

8. Emergency Preparedness:

Be prepared for unexpected health emergencies by having a basic knowledge of first aid and emergency response.

Maintain a well-stocked first aid kit at home.

9. Financial Preparedness:

Consider having health insurance and an emergency fund to address potential healthcare expenses.

Understand your healthcare coverage and explore options for financial assistance if needed.

10. Environmental Awareness:

Be aware of environmental factors that could impact health, such as air and water quality.

Take steps to minimize exposure to potential environmental hazards.

11. Stay Vaccinated:

Keep up to date with vaccinations for both common and emerging diseases. Consult with healthcare providers about the latest vaccination recommendations.

12. Telehealth Utilization:

Familiarize yourself with telehealth services for remote consultations with healthcare professionals, especially during times of health crises.

13. Community Engagement:

Engage with local health initiatives and community programs that promote wellness and disease prevention.

14. Educate Yourself:

Continuously educate yourself about health topics. Understand symptoms, risk factors, and preventive measures for various diseases.

15. Be Adaptable:

Stay flexible and adaptable in your approach to health. Be willing to adjust your lifestyle based on evolving health information.

16. Genetic Testing:

Consider genetic testing for conditions that may run in your family. This information can guide preventive measures and early detection.

17. Seek Professional Advice:

Consult with healthcare professionals regularly for personalized advice based on your health history, lifestyle, and potential risk factors.

By incorporating these practices into your lifestyle, you can enhance your overall well-being and be better prepared to face potential health challenges in the future. Remember that individual health needs may vary, and consulting with healthcare professionals is crucial for personalized guidance.

How one can time travel and why do we need

time travel:

As of our current understanding of physics and the laws of the universe, time travel, especially in the way often depicted in science fiction, remains a theoretical concept and has not been proven or achieved. In physics, time is generally considered a dimension that is closely tied to space in the fabric of spacetime. Theoretical frameworks like general relativity allow for certain solutions that could, in theory, allow time dilation, but practical time travel, as portrayed in popular culture, is not currently feasible based on our current scientific understanding.

The concept of time travel has intrigued humanity for centuries, and while we may not have achieved it, the idea has persisted in various forms. Here are some perspectives on why people might be interested in the concept of time travel:

Exploration and Discovery:

Time travel could allow for exploration of historical events or future possibilities, providing insights into the past or glimpses of potential futures.

Correction of Mistakes:

The ability to travel through time could potentially allow individuals to go back and correct mistakes, preventing negative outcomes.

Knowledge Acquisition:

Accessing different points in time could provide an opportunity to gather knowledge, technologies, or insights that may not be available in the present.

Understanding Cause and Effect:

Time travel might offer a chance to observe firsthand the cause-and-effect relationships of historical events, helping to unravel mysteries or understand the consequences of actions.

Preservation of Culture:

Time travel could be used to preserve cultural heritage, allowing people to witness and document events that might otherwise be lost to history.

Medical Applications:

The ability to manipulate time might have medical applications, allowing for the reversal of aging or the treatment of certain conditions.

Future Preparedness:

Time travel could provide a way to prepare for future challenges or disasters by gathering information about what lies ahead.

It's important to note that the concept of time travel often involves complex paradoxes, such as the famous "grandfather paradox," where traveling back in time and making changes could lead to logical contradictions. Theoretical physicists continue to explore the possibility of time travel within the framework of current scientific theories, but it remains a subject of speculation and debate.

In summary, while time travel captures the imagination and has potential philosophical and scientific implications, it is currently considered speculative and has not been realized. The exploration of such concepts often leads to interesting thought experiments and discussions about the nature of time, causality, and the limits of our understanding of the universe.

How to win success and failure how to

deal with

all this

what is a

true

failure or

success means:

Success and failure are subjective concepts that can be defined in various ways depending on individual perspectives, values, and goals. It's essential to develop a balanced and nuanced understanding of both success and failure to navigate life's challenges effectively. Here are some insights and strategies to approach success and failure:

Success:

Define Your Own Success:

Success is highly personal. It's essential to define what success means to you based on your values, aspirations, and goals.

Set Clear Goals:

Establish specific, measurable, achievable, relevant, and time-bound (SMART) goals. Clear objectives provide direction and motivation.

Celebrate Small Wins:

Acknowledge and celebrate your achievements, no matter how small. Recognizing progress boosts motivation and self-esteem.

Continuous Learning:

Success is often accompanied by a commitment to continuous learning and improvement. Embrace opportunities for growth and skill development.

Adaptability:

Be adaptable and open to adjusting your goals based on changing circumstances. Flexibility is a key aspect of long-term success.

Build a Support Network:

Surround yourself with a supportive network of friends, mentors, and colleagues. Positive relationships contribute to success.

Work Ethic and Persistence:

Cultivate a strong work ethic and be persistent in pursuing your goals. Overcoming challenges often requires determination and resilience.

Balance:

Success is holistic and includes various aspects of life, such as relationships, health, and well-being. Strive for balance rather than focusing solely on one area.

Failure:

Reframe Failure as Feedback:

View failure as an opportunity for feedback and learning. Analyze what went wrong, identify lessons, and use the experience for growth.

Learn from Mistakes:

Understand that mistakes are a natural part of the learning process. Extract valuable lessons from failures to improve future outcomes.

Resilience:

Cultivate resilience to bounce back from setbacks. Resilient individuals view challenges as temporary and develop coping strategies.

Mindset Shift:

Adopt a growth mindset. Embrace challenges and see failures as a chance to learn and improve, rather than as a reflection of your abilities.

Seek Feedback:

Seek constructive feedback from mentors, peers, or experts. External perspectives can offer valuable insights for improvement.

Redefine Success:

Challenge traditional notions of success and failure. Recognize that setbacks are not necessarily permanent and can lead to new opportunities.

Refine Strategies:

Use failure as an opportunity to reassess your strategies and approach. Adjust your plans based on lessons learned.

Maintain Perspective:

Understand that failure in one area of life does not define your overall worth or potential. Maintain a broader perspective.

True Failure and Success:

True Failure:

True failure occurs when you give up entirely, refuse to learn from mistakes, and let setbacks define your self-worth. It's a mindset that inhibits growth and progress.

True Success:

True success is not just about achieving external goals; it involves personal fulfillment, meaningful relationships, and a sense of purpose. It's a holistic and ongoing journey rather than a destination.

In summary, success and failure are complex and multifaceted aspects of life. They are not final outcomes but rather experiences that contribute to personal growth and development. Embrace both success and failure as integral parts of your journey, and use them as stepping stones toward becoming the person you aspire to be.

How to make coding easier in daily

routine or code easy daily, what things to remember

or must have in mind while coding:

Making coding easier in your daily routine involves adopting effective habits, strategies, and mindset. Here are some tips to help you code more easily and efficiently:

1. Set Clear Goals:

Define clear objectives before you start coding. Understand what you want to achieve and break down larger tasks into smaller, manageable steps.

2. Plan and Design:

Take time to plan and design your code before diving into implementation. A well-thought-out structure can make the coding process smoother.

3. Use Version Control:

Employ version control systems like Git to track changes, collaborate with others, and easily revert to previous states if needed.

4. Choose the Right Tools:

Use integrated development environments (IDEs) or code editors that suit your preferences and provide features like auto-completion, debugging tools, and syntax highlighting.

5. Stay Organized:

Organize your code into modular components or functions. Keep related code together and use clear and consistent naming conventions.

6. Comment and Document:

Add comments to explain complex sections of your code. Provide clear documentation for functions and APIs to make it easier for others (and yourself) to understand.

7. Test Regularly:

Implement testing practices, such as unit testing, to catch bugs early. Regular testing can save time in the long run by preventing issues before they escalate.

8. Continuous Learning:

Stay updated on programming languages, frameworks, and tools. Continuous learning helps you leverage new features and techniques that can simplify your coding process.

9. Code in Small Increments:

Code in small, manageable increments, and test each piece before moving on. This iterative approach can make debugging and troubleshooting more straightforward.

10. Readability Matters:

Javascript code

- Write code with readability in mind. Use consistent indentation, follow coding style guides, and choose meaningful variable and function names.

11. Avoid Overengineering:

Css code

- Keep your code simple and avoid unnecessary complexity. Overengineering can lead to more bugs and make maintenance challenging.

12. Time Management:

Css code

- Manage your time effectively by setting aside dedicated periods for coding. Avoid distractions during these focused work sessions.

13. Ask for Help:

Vbnet code

- Don't hesitate to seek help or collaborate with peers when facing challenges. Learning from others and sharing knowledge can expedite problem-solving.

14. Error Handling:

Vbnet code

- Implement robust error handling to gracefully handle unexpected situations. Log errors and provide meaningful error messages for easier debugging.

15. Code Review:

Css code

- Participate in code reviews and seek feedback from colleagues. Code reviews improve code quality, identify potential issues, and provide opportunities for learning.

16. Use Code Snippets:

Css code

- Save reusable code snippets for common tasks. This can save time and promote consistency across your projects.

17. Stay Healthy:

Vbnet code

- Take care of your physical and mental well-being. Ensure you have adequate breaks, maintain good posture, and manage stress to enhance your overall productivity.

18. Continuous Refactoring:

Css code

- Regularly refactor your code to improve its structure and readability. This ongoing process prevents the accumulation of technical debt.

19. Celebrate Small Wins:

Css code

- Acknowledge and celebrate your achievements, no matter how small. Recognizing progress boosts motivation and creates a positive coding environment.

20. Reflect and Learn from Mistakes:

Csharp code

- Reflect on your coding experiences, learn from mistakes, and continuously refine your approach. A growth mindset fosters improvement and mastery.

Remember that coding is not just about writing lines of code; it's about problem-solving, creativity, and collaboration. By incorporating these habits and strategies into your daily routine, you can make coding more enjoyable, efficient, and rewarding.

How to make mind,hear t and soul

happy overall:

Achieving overall happiness involves nurturing not just one aspect of your being but a holistic approach that encompasses your mind, heart, and soul. Here are practices that can contribute to your well-being on different levels:

Mind:

Cultivate Positive Thoughts:

Practice mindfulness to become aware of your thoughts. Replace negative thoughts with positive and constructive ones.

Continuous Learning:

Engage your mind in learning new things. This can be a new skill, a hobby, or exploring topics that interest you.

Set Realistic Goals:

Define achievable goals for personal and professional growth. Break them down into smaller, manageable steps.

Prioritize Mental Health:

Take breaks when needed, practice stress-reducing techniques, and seek professional help if you face persistent challenges.

Mindful Breathing:

Incorporate deep breathing exercises or meditation to calm your mind and reduce stress.

Heart:

Build and Maintain Relationships:

Cultivate meaningful connections with family, friends, and the community. Nurture positive and supportive relationships.

Express Gratitude:

Regularly express gratitude for the positive aspects of your life. This can be done through journaling or verbal affirmations.

Practice Empathy:

Understand and connect with the feelings of others. Practice empathy in your interactions, fostering compassion and understanding.

Forgiveness:

Release grudges and practice forgiveness. Holding onto resentment can negatively impact your emotional well-being.

Random Acts of Kindness:

Perform small acts of kindness without expecting anything in return. Acts of generosity can bring joy to both the giver and receiver.

Soul:

Find Meaning and Purpose:

Reflect on your values and beliefs. Identify activities that align with your sense of purpose and bring fulfillment.

Connect with Nature:

Spend time in nature to rejuvenate your soul. Whether it's a walk in the park or stargazing, connect with the natural world.

Mind-Body Practices:

Engage in mind-body practices like yoga or tai chi that promote harmony between your physical and spiritual self.

Explore Spirituality:

Explore spiritual practices or beliefs that resonate with you. This can involve prayer, meditation, or participating in religious or philosophical communities.

Reflect and Journal:

Take time for self-reflection. Journaling can help you explore your inner thoughts and emotions, fostering self-awareness.

Holistic Practices:

Maintain a Healthy Lifestyle:

Eat a balanced diet, engage in regular physical activity, and ensure adequate sleep. A healthy body supports a healthy mind and soul.

Disconnect and Recharge:

Take breaks from technology to disconnect from the digital world. Allow yourself moments of quiet and solitude.

Create a Joyful Environment:

Surround yourself with positive influences, whether it's through your physical surroundings, the people you spend time with, or the media you consume.

Celebrate Achievements:

Acknowledge and celebrate your achievements, both big and small. This contributes to a sense of accomplishment and happiness.

Practice Self-Compassion:

Be kind to yourself. Embrace self-compassion, understanding that everyone has flaws and experiences setbacks.

Remember that happiness is a journey rather than a destination. It involves ongoing practices and a commitment to your overall well-being. Find what works best for you, and don't hesitate to adjust your approach based on your evolving needs and circumstances.

How to live life happily:

Living a happy life involves a combination of mindset, lifestyle choices, and intentional actions. Here are some principles and practices to help you live a happier life:

1. Cultivate a Positive Mindset:

Focus on positive thoughts and gratitude. Train your mind to see the good in situations and appreciate the positive aspects of your life.

2. Set Realistic Goals:

Define clear and achievable goals for different areas of your life. Break them down into smaller, manageable steps.

3. Build Meaningful Relationships:

Cultivate strong connections with family, friends, and the community. Prioritize quality relationships that bring joy and support.

4. Practice Self-Care:

Take care of your physical, mental, and emotional well-being. Prioritize self-care activities such as exercise, proper nutrition, and sufficient sleep.

5. Live in the Present Moment:

Practice mindfulness and focus on the present moment. Enjoy and fully experience what you are doing without dwelling on the past or worrying about the future.

6. Embrace Gratitude:

Regularly express gratitude for the positive aspects of your life. Keep a gratitude journal or take time each day to reflect on the things you are thankful for.

7. Learn to Manage Stress:

Develop healthy coping mechanisms for stress. This could include relaxation techniques, deep breathing exercises, or engaging in activities that bring you peace.

8. Cultivate a Growth Mindset:

Embrace challenges as opportunities for growth. View setbacks as learning experiences rather than failures.

9. Engage in Activities You Love:

Make time for hobbies and activities that bring you joy and fulfillment. Pursuing your passions contributes to a sense of happiness and purpose.

10. Help Others:

Css code

- Practice kindness and contribute to the well-being of others. Acts of generosity and altruism can enhance your own sense of happiness.

11. Simplify Your Life:

Css code

- Declutter your physical and mental space. Simplifying your life can lead to a sense of calm and make room for what truly matters.

12. Forgive and Let Go:

Diff code

- Release grudges and forgive past hurts. Holding onto negativity can weigh you down emotionally.

13. Create and Pursue Goals:

Javascript code

- Set and pursue meaningful goals that align with your values. Achieving personal milestones can boost your sense of accomplishment.

14. Stay Active:

Css code

- Engage in regular physical activity. Exercise has been shown to release endorphins, the body's natural mood enhancers.

15. Laugh Often:

Csharp code

- Find humor in everyday situations. Laughter is a powerful stress reliever and mood booster.

16. Practice Mindful Eating:

Css code

- Pay attention to what and how you eat. Enjoy your meals mindfully, savoring the flavors and textures.

17. Limit Comparison:

Csharp code

- Avoid constant comparison with others. Focus on your own journey and celebrate your unique strengths and accomplishments.

18. Learn to Say No:

Vbnet code

- Set healthy boundaries and learn to say no when necessary. Prioritize activities and commitments that align with your values.

19. Reflect and Learn:

Csharp code

- Regularly reflect on your experiences and learn from them. Understand what brings you joy and fulfillment.

20. Seek Professional Help:

Python code

- If you're facing persistent challenges with your mental well-being, don't hesitate to seek professional help from a therapist or counselor.

Remember that happiness is a subjective and evolving concept. It's about finding a balance that aligns with your values, priorities, and unique circumstances. Be patient with yourself, and make intentional choices that contribute to your overall well-being.

Acknowledgme nts

I extend my deepest gratitude to the universe of knowledge, both real and imagined, for providing the inspiration and foundation for "Coding Cosmos: A Journey Through Time, Quantum, and Beyond."

To the pioneers of coding languages, past and present, who have shaped the landscape of technology, your innovative spirit lights the way for future coders.

A heartfelt appreciation to the quantum physicists and computer scientists pushing the boundaries of our understanding, paving the path for the exploration of QuantumScript and the mysteries of the cosmic code.

I express sincere thanks to the coding community, whose collective curiosity fuels the relentless pursuit of undiscovered languages, turning the unknown into a canvas of endless possibilities.

Special acknowledgment to the environmentalists, social activists, and humanitarian workers who showcase the tangible impact of coding on addressing present challenges, reminding us that code can be a force for positive change.

To the readers, adventurers in the coding cosmos, your curiosity and open minds are the true engines propelling this journey. May you find inspiration in every line of code and discover new horizons in the vast universe of possibilities.

Lastly, to the imaginary beings of the coding cosmos who whispered ideas into the creative process—thank you for making this exploration an imaginative and enlightening endeavor.

This book is a testament to the collaborative spirit of the coding universe, where each line of code, whether real or imagined, contributes to the symphony of knowledge and innovation.

May your coding adventures be as boundless as the cosmos.

Summary:

The book explores the integration of coding and technology into personal development, unveiling the innovative "ChronoScript" language that intertwines past and present worlds. It delves into the potential of quantum machine learning and the creation of "QuantumScript." Additionally, it introduces the excitement of deciphering undiscovered coding languages and emphasizes the positive impact of coding on present challenges. The narrative concludes by connecting coding with the universe's grand theory, urging readers to *explore limitless possibilities. This insightful journey through future coding languages encourages personal growth, technological advancement, and a holistic understanding of the cosmos.*

www.ingramcontent.com/pod-product-compliance
Lightning Source LLC
Chambersburg PA
CBHW060046260726
48658CB00004B/1203